JOHN HARBISON

CHRISTMAS VESPERS

Brass Quintet

Score and Parts

Horn in F

AMP-8034

ASSOCIATED MUSIC PUBLISHERS, Inc.

Distributed By

TWO CHORAL PRELUDES FOR ADVENT

Horn in F

John Harbison

I.

How Brightly Beams the Morning Star

47

51

55
pp

58
p

61
pp
p
mp
mf

poco rit.
65
p

II.

Come, Now, Saviour of the Heathen

for the Eastman Brass

Horn in F

The Three Wise Men

Prelude

John Harbison

* Except when notated differently, all 8/8 measures are played 2 + 3 + 3.

64
4
p
71
mf
dim.
p
77
(3+2+3)
pp
mf
83
mp
p
(3+2+3)
88
pp
94
mp
2
102
Tpt. 2
f sonoro
108
113

118
124
130
G.P.
Tbn.
138
143
chiuso
(chiuso)
150
156
3
Tpt. 1
164
aperto
171

II.

♩ = 132
mp
5
mf
f
p
9
5
pp
19
Tba.
mf
24
f
28
p
pp
III.
♩ = 132
al sord.
12
Tuba
con sord.
f
16
19
ritardando
2
mp
p
pp
via sord.

IV.

♩ = 66
senza sord.
pp
8
3
pp
cresc.
16
5
mp
mf
21
mp
p dim.
27
G.P.
pp
mf
dim.
p
V.
♩ = 132
mf
f
7
mf
f
11
mf
f
sf
dim.
15
Tuba
sf
mp
mf
22
sf
sf
mf
cresc.
27
ff
sf
sf
f
dim.
mf

VI.

𝅗𝅥 = 66
2
p
mf
p
f
8
mp
5
f
17
mf
3
ff
f cantabile
ff
23
5
f
5
28
5
mf
5
5
33
5
p
G.P.
VII.
♩ = 100
4
pp dolce
3
12
p
mp
poco marc.
18
mf
mp
p
mp
rit.
p

Postlude

28
Tbn.
mp
33
37
mf
f
f
mp
cresc.
42
ff
f
sf
sf
sf
sf
46
sf
sf
sf
sf
più f
51
mf
f
mf
più f
p
56
f
p
61
ritardando
pp

Blank for page turn.

Little Fantasy on "The Twelve Days of Christmas"

Horn in F

John Harbison

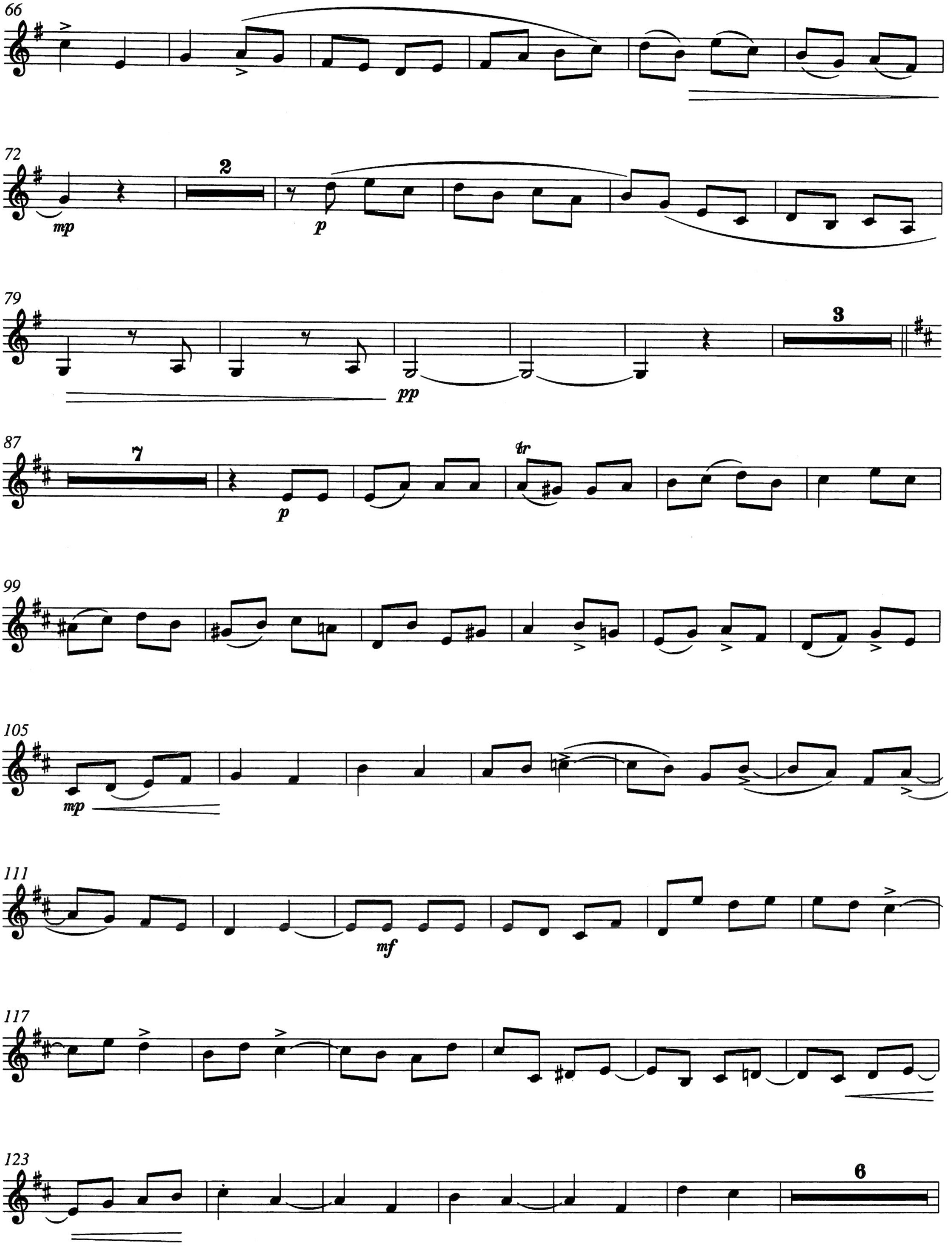
66
72
2
mp
p
79
3
pp
87
7
p
tr
99
105
mp
111
mf
117
123
6

Tpt. 2
mf
f
ff
f
Più largo
Tempo I
p
f

JOHN HARBISON

CHRISTMAS VESPERS

Brass Quintet

Score and Parts

Trombone

ASSOCIATED MUSIC PUBLISHERS, Inc.

DISTRIBUTED BY

TWO CHORAL PRELUDES FOR ADVENT

Trombone I. John Harbison

How Brightly Beams the Morning Star

39
f

ritardando
Poco meno mosso ♩ = 92
43
p dolce

47

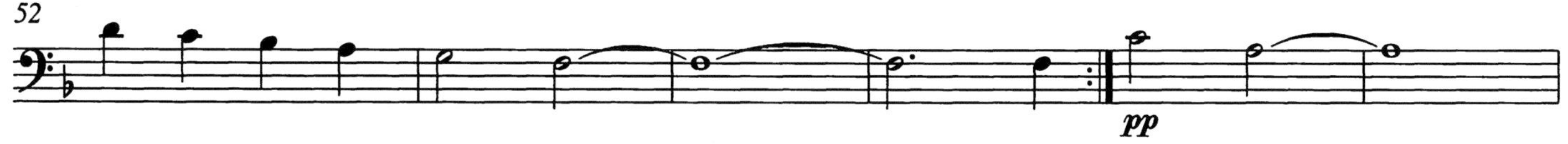
52
pp

58
p
pp
p

poco rit.
63
mp
mf
p

II.
Come, Now, Saviour of the Heathen

Moderato 𝅗𝅥 **= 60**

Tpt. 1

4

Tpt. 1

9 *ritardando* **a tempo**

14 *mf*

18 *ritardando* *p* *pp* **a tempo**

22 *mp* *mf*

27 *poco rit.* *dim.* *pp* *misterioso*

32 **a tempo** *mp*

37 *molto rit.* *poco marc.* *mf* *p*

for the Eastman Brass

Trombone

The Three Wise Men

Prelude

John Harbison

*Except where notated differently, all 8/8 measures are played 2+3+3.

72
(3+2+3)
p
cresc.
mf
78
mf
mp
84
(3+2+3)
p
90
2
p
97
mf
102
f sonoro
107
112
117

123
128
133
G.P.
con sord.
pp non stacc.
139
143
p
148
via sord.
3
senza sord.
mp
156
mf
dim.
p
4
165
mp
p
171
3
pp

Tbn.

II.

♩ = 132

mp

5 mf f p

9 pp

14 5 Tba.

23 mf

27 f

p pp

III.

al sord. ♩ = 132

Tuba

6

10 con sord.

f

14

18 ritardando

2 via sord.

mp p pp

IV.

V.

𝅗𝅥 = 66
senza sord.
pp
7
Hn. (8va)
16
mf
mp
23
p
dim.
pp
28
G.P.
mf
dim.
p
♩ = 132
mf
6
f
mf
f
10
15
Tba.
sf
mp
22
sf
mf
cresc.
27
ff
sf
sf f
dim.

VI.

𝅗𝅥 = 66

2

p mf p f

8

mp

5

f

17

mf ff

f cantabile

22

ff

5 5

f

27

5

mf

32

5

G.P.

p

VII.

♩ = 100

pp dolce

2

Tpt. 2

9

p

14

mp poco marc. mf mp

19

p mp p

rit.

Postlude

Maestoso ♩. = 84
mf
f
mp
p
dim. molto
n
Moderato comodo ♩. = 100
3
Tuba
>
mf
mp
3

Tuba
mf
f
mf
f
mp
cresc.
ff
f
sf
sf
sf
sf
sf
sf
sf
sf
più f
mf
f
mf
più f
p
f
p
ritardando
pp

Blank for page turn.

Little Fantasy on "The Twelve Days of Christmas"

Trombone

John Harbison

66
mp
72
p
6
mp
78
7
Hn.
7
Tpt. 2
8
mp
113
mf
120
127
133
140
146
mf

152
4
f
161
167
ff
174
tr
f
180
187
Più largo
p
193
Tempo I
199
pp
f

JOHN HARBISON

CHRISTMAS VESPERS

Brass Quintet

Score and Parts

Tuba

ASSOCIATED MUSIC PUBLISHERS, Inc.

TWO CHORAL PRELUDES FOR ADVENT

Tuba

I.

How Brightly Beams the Morning Star

John Harbison

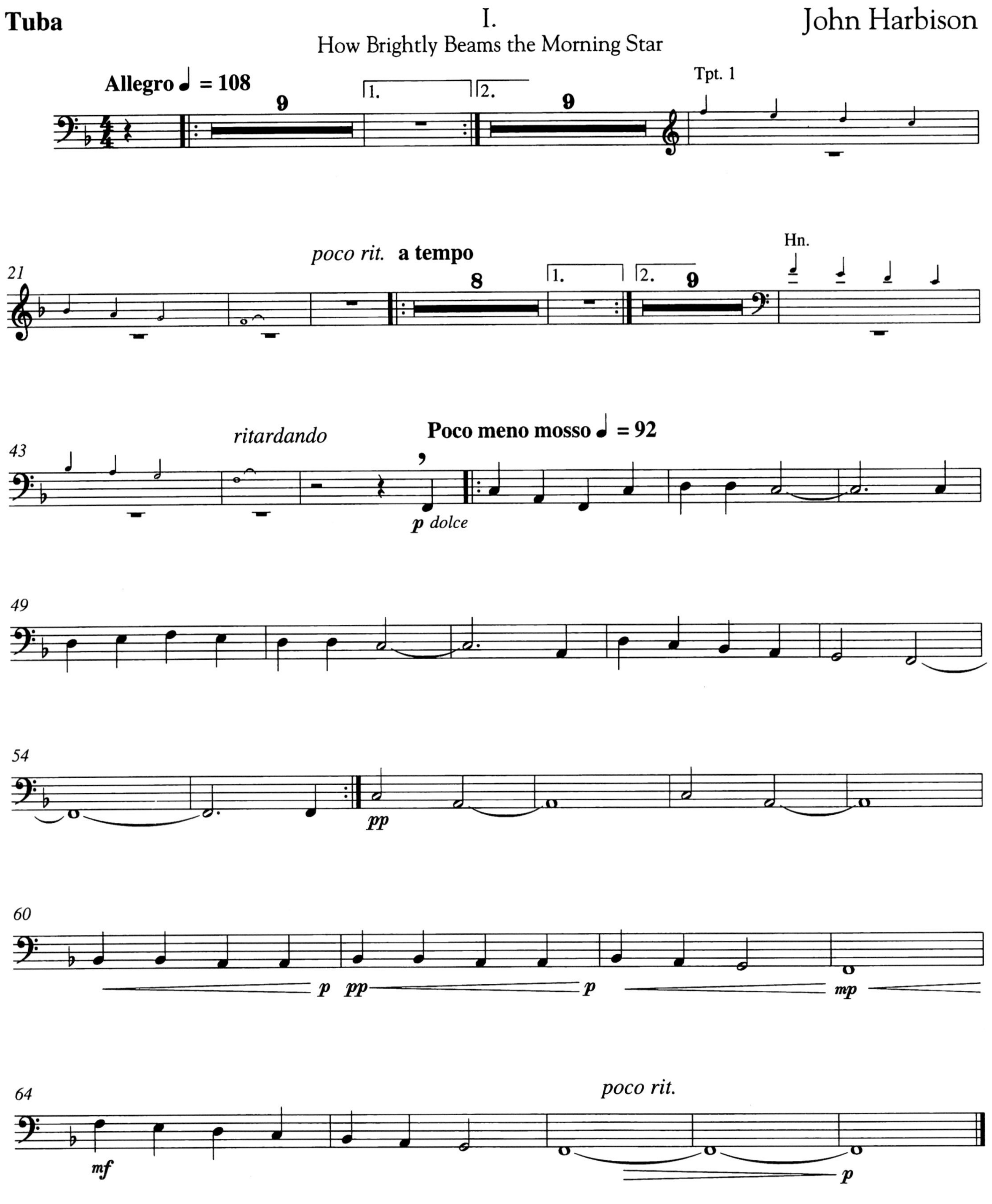

II.

Come, Now, Saviour of the Heathen

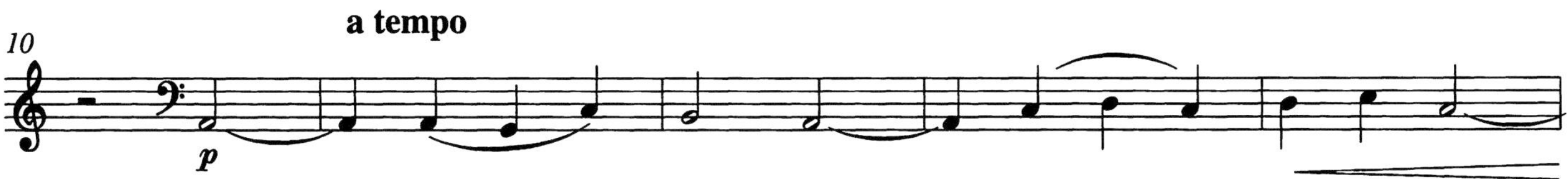

Tuba

for the Eastman Brass

The Three Wise Men

Prelude

John Harbison

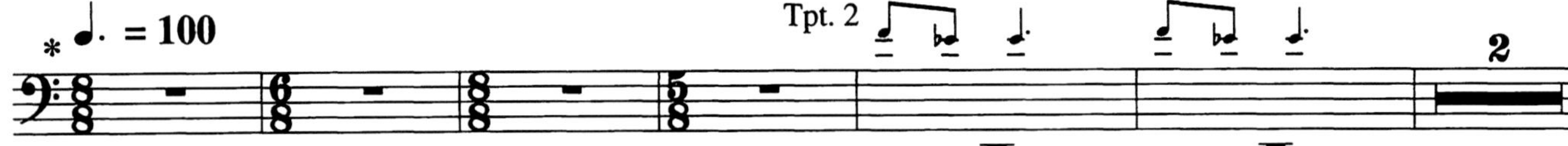

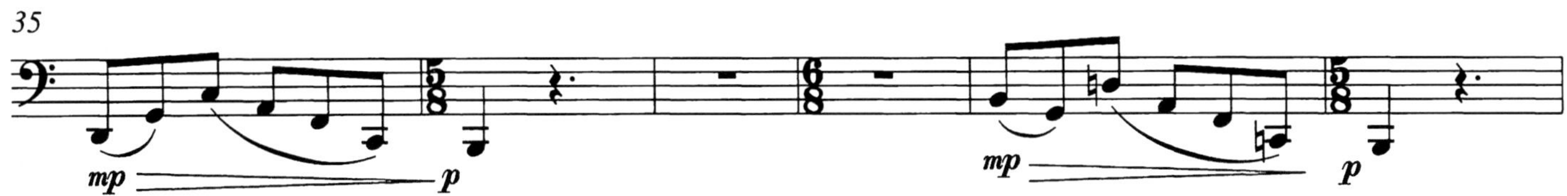

* Except where notated differently, all 8/8 measures are played 2+3+3.

47
sf
fsf
52
sf
sf
57
mf
63
mp
p
pp
69
5
(3+2+3)
80
Tbn.
mp
p
86
(3+2+3)
2
Tpt 1. (8va)

93
p
mf
101
f sonoro
108
115
123
131
G.P.
Tbn.
Tpt. 1
142
3
2
3
Tbn.
157
mf
mp
dim.
p
pp
2
166
mp
2
p
3
pp

II.
♩ = 132
Tpt. 1 (8va)
Tpt. 2 (8va)
17
21
dim.
III.
♩ = 132
5
10
15
19
ritardando
dim.
dim.

Tuba

IV.

♩ = 66
pp
7
5
Hn. (8va)
4
mf
21
mp
5
p
dim.
27
pp
G.P.
mf
dim.
p
V.
♩ = 132
3
f
sfp
fp
5
9
Tpt. 1 (8va)
2
19
dim.
23
p
pp
mf

9

VI.
Tacet
= 66
2
Tbn.
34

VII.

= 100
pp misterioso

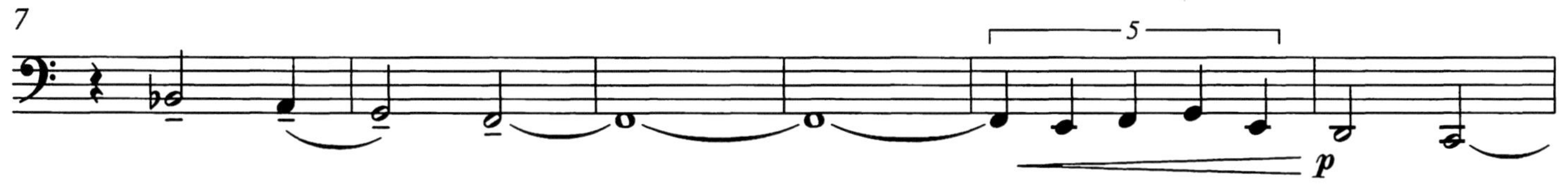
7
5
p

13
5
3
mp
dim.

19
rit.
p

Tuba

Postlude

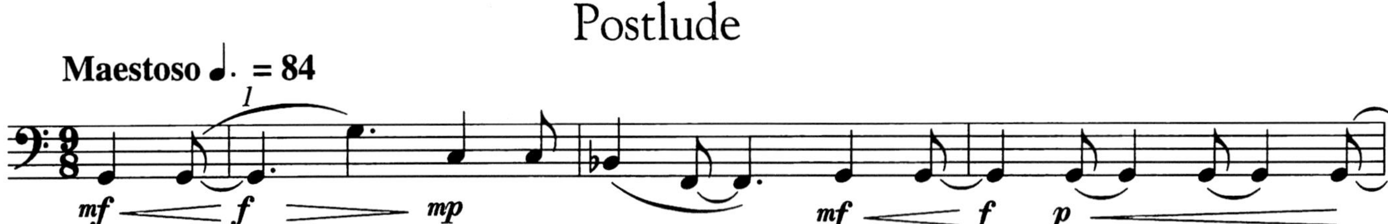

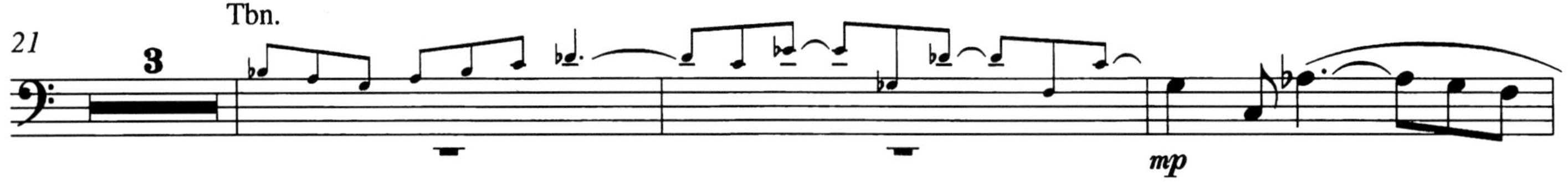

31
mp
35
mf
39
f
mf
f
mp
cresc.
ff
44
f
sf
sf
sf
sf
sf
sf
sf
sf
48
più f
mf
f
53
mf
più f
p
f
57
p
62
ritardando
pp

Tuba

Little Fantasy on "The Twelve Days of Christmas"

John Harbison

Giocoso, molto allegro
♩ = 152

A Tbn. mp p

B pp

C mp mf f sf

mf

mp p

pp mp p

tr

leggiero

101
mp
108
15
Tpt. 2
130
f
138
145
6
mf
13
169
mf
ff
f
177
185
Più largo
p
Tempo I
193
5
pp
f